09743

Let's Build a Rocket

DEER PARK SCHOOL WINGERWORTH

Written by Nicole Sharrocks
Illustrated by T. S. Spookytooth

 Collins

I'm building a rocket,
as soon as I'm done,

2

I'm taking my friends
on a trip to the Sun.

But what do you mean
that the Sun is too hot?

Oh well, I suppose
I'll just pick a new spot.

I'm building a rocket,
I'm finishing soon,

and I'm taking my friends on a trip to the Moon!

But what do you mean that the Moon has no air?

Oh well, I suppose
I'll just pick a new spot.

9

I'm building a rocket,
it's going to fly,

I'm taking my friends
way up high.

But what do you mean
when you ask how will it land?

This rocket is harder
to build than
I planned.

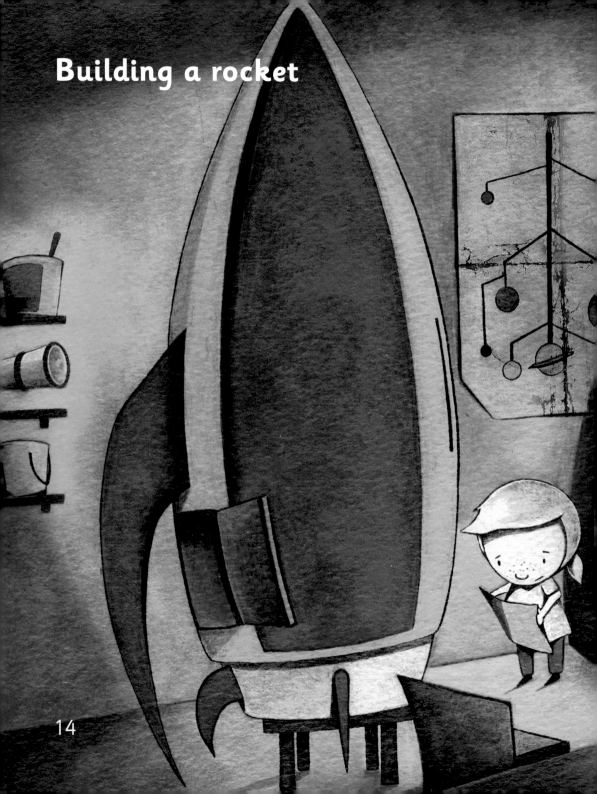

Building a rocket

Ideas for reading

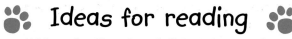

Written by Clare Dowdall BA(Ed), MA(Ed)
Lecturer and Primary Literacy Consultant

Learning objectives: use phonics to read unknown or difficult words; read automatically high frequency words; identify the main events and characters in stories; explore the effect of patterns of language and repeated words and phrases; comment on events, characters and ideas, making imaginative links to own experiences; retell stories ordering events using story language

Curriculum links: Science: Light and dark

High frequency words: I'm, a, as, my, on, to, the, but, what, do, you, that, is, too, just, new, and, has, no, it, going, way, up, when, how, will, this, than

Interest words: build, rocket, sun, moon, air, high

Resources: collage materials, e.g. card, shiny paper and glue

Word count: 115

Getting started

- Ask children if they have seen a space rocket in a picture, film or story. Help children to describe what a space rocket is like and what it is used for.

- Read the title and blurb aloud together. Help children to read with expression, emphasising the title. Explain that this book is a poem, and that it might have rhythm and a rhyming pattern.

- Show children the interest words using flashcards. Model how to read them using phonic knowledge and other strategies, e.g. looking for words within words and using the context.

Reading and responding

- Walk through the book together. Ask children to find the interest words and discuss what is happening in each picture, e.g. on pp4–5 the children are uncomfortable because it's too hot.

- Discuss how to use the question mark on p4 to add interest.